CHAMPIONING CHANGE

KEVIN EIKENBERRY

Participant Workbook

Pfeiffer
A Wiley Imprint
www.pfeiffer.com

Participant Workbook ISBN 978-0-470-50183-2
Facilitator's Guide Set ISBN 978-0-470-50557-1

Acquiring Editor: Holly J. Allen   Developmental Editor: Susan Rachmeler
Assistant Editor: Lindsay Morton   Production Editor: Michael Kay
Marketing Manager: Tolu Babalola   Manufacturing Supervisor: Becky Morgan
Director of Development: Kathleen Dolan Davies

Printed in the United States of America
Printing   10 9 8 7 6 5 4 3 2 1

Contents

THE COMPETENCIES OF REMARKABLE LEADERS

The Remarkable Leadership workshop series is based on the book *Remarkable Leadership: Unleashing Your Leadership Potential One Skill at a Time* and consists of twelve workshops, based on thirteen leadership competencies from the book. (There is no workshop for the first competency, learn continually, as that competency is embedded in all the workshops.) Although you may not be attending the full series of workshops, all thirteen competencies are listed next.

Remarkable Leaders . . .

1. Learn Continually

2. **Champion Change**

3. Communicate Powerfully

4. Build Relationships

5. Develop Others

6. Focus on Customers

7. Influence with Impact

8. Think and Act Innovatively

9. Value Collaboration and Teamwork

10. Solve Problems and Make Decisions

11. Take Responsibility/Accountability

12. Manage Projects and Processes Successfully

13. Set Goals and Support Goal Setting

After completing this workshop, you will

- Understand the factors that affect how people respond to change.

- Have a process you can follow to develop change plans.

- Have nine specific tactics you can employ to champion change.

Ponder, and then write your answers to the following questions:

1. What do I hope to gain in this session?

2. What are my experiences with change at work?

3. What types of changes have I accepted or embraced?

4. What changes have I resisted?

5. What is the difference between these two lists?

SELF-ASSESSMENT

Here is a quick assessment to help you think about how effectively you understand, lead, and champion change.

Use the following 1–7 scale on each question:

1 – Almost never	5 – Usually
2 – Rarely/Seldom	6 – Frequently
3 – Occasionally	7 – Almost always
4 – Sometimes	

I see the positive in changes I'm involved in.   ___

I understand organizational change.   ___

I recognize the forces that impact change.   ___

I create and share a vision of the future
as change is implemented.   ___

I adapt to change easily.   ___

I support organizational changes.   ___

I deal with resistance productively.   ___

Synonyms

- addition
- advance
- conversion
- innovation
- revolution
- transformation
- variation

- adjustment
- break
- diversification
- refinement
- shift
- transition

Other Words Associated with Change

- dread
- fear
- progress
- too fast
- uncertainty

- excitement
- needed
- too expensive
- too soon

What words would you add to these lists?

FACTORS THAT DRIVE OUR FEELINGS TOWARD CHANGE

It is about feelings!

■ Experience

■ Relative (and recent) success (or failure)

■ Context

■ Perceived risk/reward

■ Habits

The Diffusion of Innovation

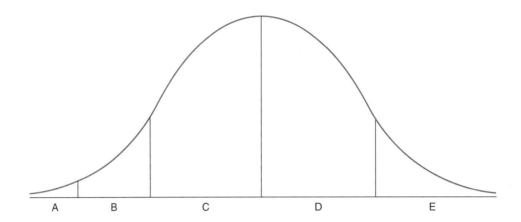

A. _____—only _____% of the population.

  • Most willing to take risk.

B. Early _____—about _____% of the population.

  • On the leading edge of change.

C. Early _____—about _____% of the population.

  • More deliberate and watchful.

D. Late _____—about _____% of the population.

  • Still more deliberate. Possibly skeptical, especially at the beginning of a change.

E. _____—about _____% of the population.

  • Sometimes viewed as hostile to our unwilling to change. Will be the most deliberate and cautious. Generally need to learn from the direct experience of people they trust.

SOME OBSERVATIONS ABOUT THE DIFFUSION OF INNOVATION

- No "wrong" group
- Habits play a role
- Use this knowledge to help you lead change

What are the practical implications?

Timing and Targets

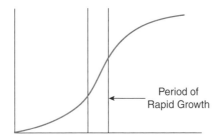

Parts of a Change Plan

1. Create dissatisfaction.

2. Create a vision.

3. Identify steps to move forward.

4. Identify how to minimize risks/costs.

■ Direction of Communication

- More _____-way than _____-way

- More conversation than PowerPoint

- More one-on-one than one-to-many

- Earlier rather than later

■ Frequency of Communication

- More frequent than you think is necessary

- Share what you know when you know it

- Don't wait to have all the details first

MANAGE, LEAD, OR CHAMPION?

Manage	Lead	Champion
administer	steer	support
run	shepherd	advocate
supervise	move	believe
organize	convey	nurture

1. Which do I do?

2. Which has the best chance for organizational success?

3. Why?

Communicating About Change

Change Leaders . . .	Change Champions . . .
Focus on the change	Focus on the people
Focus on the change	Focus on the vision
Communicate about the change	Create dialogue about the change

So, Change Champions . . .

- Communicate emotions

- Show belief in the change

- Show enthusiasm

  - IASM = _____ _____ _____ _____

■ "Sell" _____.

• How can you get past the crowd to speak with individuals?

■ Help people take _____.

• What can you do to engage people so that they "own" the change?

■ Let people _____ your process.

• How can you be transparent? What can you do to stop the negative gossip by sharing what you know?

- Talk about change as a _____.

  - What words or images can you use to communicate the change as a journey rather than a destination?

- _____ questions.

  - What types of questions can you ask, and whom can you ask them of to engage people in a dialogue about the change?

- Start _____—build a new status quo.

  - Which small step can you take to get a win? How can you build positive momentum on your change journey?

- Give it _____.

  - What words do you use to describe the change journey? What words describe your vision? How can you communicate these words so that everyone is speaking the same language?

- _____ questions.

  - Yes, we already mentioned this tactic. It's worth repeating. Use more questions and dialogue and fewer statements and monologue.

- Take _____.

  - How can you demonstrate that you take responsibility for the change without robbing your team of ownership? What positive steps can you take to show your commitment to the change?

Planning Change Efforts

1. Talk to someone you think is typically in a different category on the Diffusion of Innovation curve than you. What can you learn from this other perspective?

2. Explore this person's feelings and experiences with change. Work to understand what motivates this person to change and what information lowers the costs and risks in his or her mind. How does this person view change differently from you?

3. How can you use these insights the next time you are planning a change?

Being a Change Champion

1. Review the twelve verbs in the table on page 12. What do you see?

2. Reflect on which of these actions you are most comfortable with and likely best at. Capture your initial thoughts here, and continue the process in your journal.

3. Next, select another verb from the list you would like to do more effectively. Write that new target skill here if you don't have a leadership journal.

4. Think about your next change opportunity, and identify two things you will do to help you execute the new skill you have identified. Put your ideas and next steps here or in your journal.

1. Think back to your goals for being here (page 3). Reflect on what you have learned that you can apply to your situation.

2. Teach a colleague (or your team) the content we discussed today as a way to solidify your own knowledge and understanding. What do you plan to teach? Who do you plan to teach it to?

3. Be responsible for applying these concepts and ideas in your work and the rest of your life. How can you keep these concepts at the forefront of your mind in the future?

4. Ask yourself: "Which Now Steps will I apply *right now?*"

5. Take those actions!

6. Commit to your daily application to lock in your learning and achieve greater results!

"We move toward our potential when we turn learning into action."

~Kevin Eikenberry

More tips on Championing Change can be found at **www.RLBonus.com.**

- To get some specific help on making the vision personal, use the keywords "personal vision."

- To learn more about the diffusion of innovation and how it can affect your change plans, use the keyword "diffusion."